First World War
and Army of Occupation
War Diary
France, Belgium and Germany

30 DIVISION
Divisional Troops
South Wales Borderers
6th Battalion
1 June 1918 - 30 June 1919

WO95/2323/4

Published by

The Naval & Military Press Ltd

Unit 10 Ridgewood Industrial Park,

Uckfield, East Sussex,

TN22 5QE England

Tel: +44 (0) 1825 749494

www.naval-military-press.com

www.nmarchive.com

This diary has been reprinted in facsimile from the original. Any imperfections are inevitably reproduced and the quality may fall short of modern type and cartographic standards.

© **Crown Copyright**
Images reproduced by permission of The National Archives, London, England, 2015.

Contents

Document type	Place/Title	Date From	Date To
Heading	6th Bn Sth Wales Bordrs June 1918-June 1919 2323/4		
Heading	30th Division Divl Troops 6th Bn Sth Wales Bordrs (Pioneers) Jun 1918-June 1919 From 25 Division Troops		
War Diary	Loisy En Brie Ref. Map Sheet Arcis 1/80.000	01/06/1918	07/06/1918
War Diary	Loisy En Brie	08/06/1918	09/06/1918
War Diary	St Loup	10/06/1918	19/06/1918
War Diary	Vindey	20/06/1918	30/06/1918
Miscellaneous	Headquarters "A" 30th (British) Division	06/08/1918	06/08/1918
War Diary	Vindey	01/07/1918	01/07/1918
War Diary	Pleurs	02/07/1918	02/07/1918
War Diary	Gourgancon	03/07/1918	03/07/1918
War Diary	Mailly-Le-Camp	04/07/1918	04/07/1918
War Diary	Pont Remy	05/07/1918	05/07/1918
War Diary	Sorel	06/07/1918	07/07/1918
War Diary	Clairmarais	08/07/1918	09/07/1918
War Diary	Bavinchove	10/07/1918	11/07/1918
War Diary	Oxelaere	12/07/1918	13/07/1918
War Diary	Boeschepe Area	14/07/1918	25/07/1918
War Diary	None Bosch	26/07/1918	31/07/1918
Miscellaneous	Headquarters, 30th British Division. A.	03/09/1918	03/09/1918
War Diary	None Bosch	01/08/1918	05/08/1918
War Diary	Oxelaere	06/08/1918	09/08/1918
War Diary	Westoutre Area	10/08/1918	31/08/1918
Miscellaneous	Report On Operations Carried Out By The 6th (S). Battalion, South Wales Borderers, (Pioneers)., On the night	22/08/1918	22/08/1918
Miscellaneous	Report On Operations Carried Out By The 6th (S). Battalion, South Wales Borderers, (Pioneers)., On the night	21/08/1918	21/08/1918
Miscellaneous	Report On Operations Carried Out By The 6th (S). Battalion, South Wales Borderers, (Pioneers)., On the night	20/08/1918	20/08/1918
War Diary	Westoutre	01/09/1918	03/09/1918
War Diary	Locre	04/09/1918	08/09/1918
War Diary	Kemmel	09/09/1918	30/09/1918
Miscellaneous	Headquarters, 30th British Division. "A"	01/11/1918	01/11/1918
War Diary	Field	01/10/1918	31/10/1918
Miscellaneous	30th Division No. A/9568	16/12/1918	16/12/1918
Heading	War Diary For Month Of November 1918 6th Bn South Wales Borderers Vol 43		
War Diary	Farm 2000x N.E. of Saint-Genois	01/11/1918	03/11/1918
War Diary	Knokke	09/11/1918	10/11/1918
War Diary	Avelghem	11/11/1918	11/11/1918
War Diary	Amougies	12/11/1918	12/11/1918
War Diary	Watripont	13/11/1918	13/11/1918
War Diary	Anseroel	13/11/1918	17/11/1918
War Diary	Heestert	18/11/1918	18/11/1918
War Diary	Aelbeke	19/11/1918	30/11/1918

Heading	War Diary 6th South Wales Borders For December 1918 Vol 44		
War Diary	Linselles	01/12/1918	01/12/1918
War Diary	Funquereau	02/12/1918	02/12/1918
War Diary	Lagorgue	03/12/1918	03/12/1918
War Diary	St. Venant	04/12/1918	04/12/1918
War Diary	Ebblinghem	05/12/1918	31/12/1918
Miscellaneous	Headquarters "A" 30th Division	31/01/1919	31/01/1919
War Diary	Dunkirk	01/01/1919	28/02/1919
Heading	War Diary Of 6th Bn South Wales Bdrs For February 1919		
Miscellaneous	Headquarters "A" 30th (British) Division.	02/04/1919	02/04/1919
War Diary	Dunkirk	01/03/1919	25/03/1919
War Diary	Ecault	26/03/1919	31/03/1919
Miscellaneous	Headquarters "A" 30th Division.	03/05/1919	03/05/1919
War Diary	Ecault	01/04/1919	31/05/1919
Heading	War Diary Of 6th S.W.B For May 1919		
War Diary	Ecault.	01/06/1919	06/06/1919
War Diary	Henriville Camp	07/06/1919	30/06/1919
Heading	War Diary Of 6th Bn South Wales Borders For June 1919		

2323/W4

6TH BN STH WALES BORDAS

JUNE 1918 — JUNE 1919

30TH DIVISION
DIVL TROOPS

6TH BN STH WALES BORDRS
(PIONEERS)
JUN 1918 - JUN 1919

from 25 DIVISION TROOPS

Army Form C. 2118.

WAR DIARY
of 4th/6(5)/Bn: SOUTH WALES BORDERERS PIONEERS
INTELLIGENCE SUMMARY.

(Erase heading not required.)

Instructions regarding War Diaries and Intelligence Summaries are contained in F. S. Regs., Part II. and the Staff Manual respectively. Title pages will be prepared in manuscript.

Place	Date June	Hour	Summary of Events and Information	Remarks and references to Appendices
LOISY EN BRIE Ref. Map Sheet ARCIS 1/86,450	1st	10pm	**COMMAND** Maj. A REID-KELLETT M.C. assumed command of the Bn. vice Lt. Col. L.C.W. Deane D.S.O. M.C. killed in action as from the 29/5/18. Bn. trained as per programme.	A.
do	2nd		**COMMAND** Maj. W.L. CRAWFORD D.S.O. having reported for duty assumes command of the Bn. as from today. Bn. trained; Open order fighting. Fire Control. Extending & advancing. Lewis Gunners & Signallers under respective instructors.	A.
do	3rd		Batt. trained as per Bn. scheme.	A. A.
do	4th		Bn. trained; Musketry. Open order fighting. Gas Drill etc. also Pioneer training; digging, knotts making etc. etc.	A.
do	5th		Batt. trained as per Bn. scheme.	A. A.
do	6th		Batt. carried out Infantry Training.	A.
do	7th		Batt. trained as follows Physical Training. Open Order fighting. Gas Drill. Pioneer Training etc. etc.	A.

Army Form C. 2118.

WAR DIARY
or
INTELLIGENCE SUMMARY.
(Erase heading not required.)

Instructions regarding War Diaries and Intelligence Summaries are contained in F. S. Regs., Part II. and the Staff Manual respectively. Title pages will be prepared in manuscript.

Place	Date June	Hour	Summary of Events and Information	Remarks and references to Appendices
LOISY EN BRIE	8th		Bn. trained as per Bn. Scheme	R.
do	9th		Bn. moved by march route to ST LOUP arriving there at 3.15 P.M.	R.
ST LOUP	10th		Bn. trained as per Bn. Scheme	R.
do	11th		Bn. trained as by Coys. Infantry & Lewis Training	R.
do	12th		COMMAND. MAJ. N.G. PEARSON D.S.O. M.C. assumes the duties of Second in Command of the Bn. as from June 3rd 1918. CAPT. D.H. STICKLER M.C. takes over Command and Payment of 'A' Coy as from the same date. WORK. 'A' Coy. worked on Construction of Rifle Range under orders of O.C. 105th Coy R.E. about two Kilos. S.E. of ALLEMANT. 'D' Coy. worked on the repair of ST LOUP - ALLEMANT Road. Remaining Coys. also Lewis Gunners & Signallers trained as per programme.	R. R.
do	13th		'A' Coy. 30 men of C' Coy. continued work on Rifle Range 'D' Coy and C' Coy less 30 men to 'A' Coy. continued work on ST LOUP - ALLEMANT Road. Lewis Gunners & Signallers carried out training as usual.	R. R.

(A9175) Wt. W3358/930 60,000 12/17 D. D. & L. Sch. 5za. Forms/C2118/15

WAR DIARY
INTELLIGENCE SUMMARY.
(Erase heading not required.)

Army Form C. 2118.

Place	Date June	Hour	Summary of Events and Information	Remarks and references to Appendices
St LOUP	14		**WORK** Coy. continues work on R. Range. 'C' Coy in addition sent 50 men to report to G.O.C. 75th Inf. Bde. at 9.30 am 'D' Coy. continues work on road as for yesterday. Specialists parade as for yesterday under instructors. 2/Lt. L. PETTS M.C. 4/m Officer is appointed Assistant Adjutant as from the 12th inst.	R. R.
do	15		The P/m Officers having reported for duty are taken on the strength and posted to Coys as follows:- 2/Lt WILLIAMSON C — 'A' Coy. 2/Lt TOWNSEND E — 'D' Coy. **WORK** One Officer & 20 men of 'A' Coy. continues work on Range. 'D' Coy continues work on road as for yesterday. Remainder of Bn. continued training as per Bn. programme.	R.
do	16		Bn. paraded at 11.5 am for Divine Service. R.Cs at 10.30 am. Non Conformists at 10.30 am.	R.

(9173) Wt W2355/P360 50000 12/7 D.D.&L. Sch 5Bs. Forms/C2118/5.

Army Form C. 2118.

WAR DIARY
or
INTELLIGENCE SUMMARY.
(Erase heading not required.)

Instructions regarding War Diaries and Intelligence Summaries are contained in F. S. Regs., Part II. and the Staff Manual respectively. Title pages will be prepared in manuscript.

Place	Date June	Hour	Summary of Events and Information	Remarks and references to Appendices
ST LOUP	17		Bn. less Signallers & Lewis Gunners paraded at 8 am for ROUTE MARCH. Strict attention being paid to March Discipline. Specialists paraded and trained under instructors.	A.
do.	18		COMMAND MAJ. A. REID-KELLETT MC. having rejoined the Bn. this day, takes over duties of Second in Command from Maj. N.G. PEARSON DSO, MC. HONOURS AND AWARDS The Corps Commander has, under authority delegated to him, awarded the following decorations:— THE MILITARY MEDAL 53953 Sgt. COOPER J. DCM. 6/29046 L. PRINCE I. 6/19383 Cpl. GOTH W. 17086 Pte CATEWELL F. 40851 - BEARD A. 17477 -	

WAR DIARY
or
INTELLIGENCE SUMMARY.
(Erase heading not required.)

Army Form C. 2118.

Place	Date	Hour	Summary of Events and Information	Remarks and references to Appendices
ST LOUP	18		Bn. trained as per Bn. programme	R.
do	19		Bn. trained as per Bn. Scheme. Lectures on Pioneering given in afternoon.	R.
VINDEY	20		Bn. moved by march route to VINDEY ref. sheet ARCIS. arriving there by 12 NOON.	R.
do	21		Boys carried out training as per programme. Signallers to Lewis Gunners trained under instructors. (ATTACHMENT) CAPT. G.T. MACLEAN R.A.M.C. having reported to-day takes over duties of Medical Officer in charge of Unit - vice CAPT. A.C. MANN M.C. R.A.M.C. admitted to hospital.	R.
do	22		Boys trained under their own arrangements and specialists under Gun instructors.	R.
do	23		The G.O.C. 50TH Div. inspected the Bn. at 4 P.M.	R.
do	24		Bn. trained under Coy. arrangements. Specialists under instructors.	R.
do	25		Bn. trained under Coy arrangements. Specialists under instructors	Appx.
do	26		Orders received to be prepared to move to a new area. Transport	

WAR DIARY
or
INTELLIGENCE SUMMARY.
(Erase heading not required.)

Army Form C. 2118.

Place	Date	Hour	Summary of Events and Information	Remarks and references to Appendices
VINDEY	26		Moved at 10 A.M. Battalion ready in preparation for the move the following day. 2 the moving information was received that the move had been cancelled.	appx
do.	27		Transport rejoined the Battalion. Companies carried out training under Coy arrangements. Schedule made instructing Coy arrangements	appx
do.	28		Companies carried out training under instruction Specialists under instruction	appx
do.	29.		Companies training during the morning, made company arrangements. Lewis gunners fired on the range near SAUDOY.	appx
do	30.		Battalion resting. Warning orders issued reference move tomorrow	appx

W.R. Crawford Lt. Col.,
Commdg. 6(S) Bn. South Wales Borderers (?)

To:-

    HEADQUARTERS "A",

        30th (BRITISH) DIVISION.

    Herewith WAR DIARY of the 6th Battalion South Wales Borderers (Pioneers) for the month of JULY 1918.

6. 8. 18.
    6th BATTALION SOUTH WALES BORDERERS (PIONEERS).
                                    CAPT. & ADJT.

Army Form C. 2118.

WAR DIARY or INTELLIGENCE SUMMARY. 6(S) Bn. SOUTH WALES BORDERERS PNRS

Vol 35

(Erase heading not required.)

Instructions regarding War Diaries and Intelligence Summaries are contained in F. S. Regs., Part II. and the Staff Manual respectively. Title pages will be prepared in manuscript.

Place	Date	Hour	Summary of Events and Information	Remarks and references to Appendices
VINDEY	1/7/18		Battalion moved by march route to PLEURS, marching at 1.15 pm. Very hot marching	
PLEURS	2/7/18		Battalion moved by march route to GOURGANÇON, marching at 8.30 am	
GOURGANÇON	3/7/18		Battalion moved by march route to MAILLY-LE-CAMP and occupied huts E. of the Camp. marching at 3.30 pm.	
MAILLY-LE-CAMP	4/7/18		"A" "B" and "C" Coys with Battalion H.Q commenced entraining with 1 Battalion transport at 2.30 am. Left MAILLY-LE-CAMP at 4.52 am. "D" Coy and ½ Transport under Major A. Reid. KCIE MC commenced entraining at 5.30am & left MAILLY-LE-CAMP at 5.30 am for PONT REMY.	

Army Form C. 2118.

WAR DIARY
or
INTELLIGENCE SUMMARY.
(Erase heading not required.)

Instructions regarding War Diaries and Intelligence Summaries are contained in F. S. Regs., Part II. and the Staff Manual respectively. Title pages will be prepared in manuscript.

Place	Date	Hour	Summary of Events and Information	Remarks and references to Appendices
PONT REMY	5/2/18		1st H.Q. Coy. and 2 Transport detrained at 6 am & marched to Billets at SOREL.	
SOREL	6/2/18		A & D Coy and 2 Transport detrained at 8.30 am marched to Billets at SOREL	
SOREL	7/2/18		Kit Inspection. Training carried out as usual.	
			Battalion Complete entrained at 2 pm at PONT REMY and proceeded to ST OMER detraining at 10 pm and marched to bivouacs at CLAIRMARAIS	
CLAIRMARAIS	8/2/18		Kit Inspection only and Physical Training. Batt n rested.	
do	9/2/18		Battalion marched under orders of 21st Infantry Brigade to BAVINCHOVE and went into billets	
BAVINCHOVE	10/2/18		Battalion trained under Company arrangements. Specialists trained under their various instructors	

Army Form C. 2118.

WAR DIARY
or
INTELLIGENCE SUMMARY.
(Erase heading not required.)

Instructions regarding War Diaries and Intelligence Summaries are contained in F. S. Regs., Part II. and the Staff Manual respectively. Title pages will be prepared in manuscript.

Place	Date	Hour	Summary of Events and Information	Remarks and references to Appendices
BAVINCHOVE	11/7/18		Battalion moved to OXELAERE area to billet. G.O.C. 30th Division saw all officers of the Battalion at Batt:n H.Q. at 5pm and inspected some of the billets	
OXELAERE	12/7/18		2nd in Command & O's C. "A" & "D" Coy Reconnoitred area between GODEWAERSVELDE and BOESCHEPE for accommodation for the Battalion. Company's carried out training under Company arrangements	
do	13/7/18		Warning order received to be prepared to move to the forward area. Advance party which went into the billets retained to the Battalion as the billets were not available	
BOESCHEPE AREA	14/7/18		Battalion moved at 1.30 pm from OXELAERE via STEENVOORDE & GODEWAERSVELDE to bivouac at R.9.a.2.3 West of BOESCHEPE. Very little cover was available and the men got very wet before shelter could be found	

Army Form C. 2118.

WAR DIARY
or
INTELLIGENCE SUMMARY.

(Erase heading not required.)

Instructions regarding War Diaries and Intelligence Summaries are contained in F. S. Regs., Part II. and the Staff Manual respectively. Title pages will be prepared in manuscript.

Place	Date	Hour	Summary of Events and Information	Remarks and references to Appendices
BOESCHEPE AREA	15/7/18		Battalion Commenced work on the Army Line at 4 a.m. Digging & wiring	
do	16/7/18		Battalion at work on the Army Line. Bivouacs Tents received from Corps.	
do	17/7/18		Battalion at work on the Army Line. At 11 p.m. the Battalion moved to take up defensive positions in the Army Line	
do	18/7/18		At 5 a.m. Battalion returned from the Army Line and rested	
do	19/7/18		Battalion at work on the Army Line	
do	20/7/18		Battalion at work on the Army Line	
do	21/7/18		Battalion at work on the Army Line	

Army Form C. 2118.

WAR DIARY
or
INTELLIGENCE SUMMARY.
(Erase heading not required.)

Instructions regarding War Diaries and Intelligence Summaries are contained in F. S. Regs., Part II. and the Staff Manual respectively. Title pages will be prepared in manuscript.

Place	Date	Hour	Summary of Events and Information	Remarks and references to Appendices
BOESCHEPE AREA	22/7/18		Batt". at work on the Army Line	M
do	23/7/18		Batt". at work on the Army Line	M
do	24/7/18		Batt". at work on the Army Line	M
do	25/7/18		At 12.30pm orders were received from 8 Corps that the Batt". would vacate its present bivouacs at R.9.a.2.5 BOESCHEPE AREA and move to HONE BOSCH WOOD. The move was carried out as follows. H.Q. moved at 5pm. Companies remained and after work had ceased to stack their packs for removal the following day. The G.O.C 30th British Division visited the Camp	M
HONE BOSCH	26/7/18		Companies proceeded to work on the Army Line at 2.30am and after work hole converged by train to the new area by Light Railway. The difficulty in pitching Stores Camp was very great owing to the tremendous amount of rain.	M

WAR DIARY
or
INTELLIGENCE SUMMARY.
(Erase heading not required.)

Army Form C. 2118.

Place	Date	Hour	Summary of Events and Information	Remarks and references to Appendices
NONE BOSCH	27/2/18		The Battalion proceeded to work on the Army Line entraining at NONE BOSCH Siding at 2.30 am and detraining at LOYE, returning by Light Railway. Entrained at LOYE at 7.30 am	
do	28/2/18		Battalion proceeded to work on Army Line entraining to & from LOYE as yesterday. The 2nd Batt: Hampshire Regt: detailed to work under this Battalion were also at work digging on the Army Line	
do	29/2/18		The Battalion at work on the Army Line proceeding to & from LOYE by train. The 2nd Hampshires also at work on the Line	
do	30/2/18		The Battalion at work on the Army Line also the 2nd Hampshires. D Company have been detailed to take over from the R.E's of the 29th Division, a battle track running along the Corps N boundary proceed with its construction	

Place	Date	Hour	Summary of Events and Information	Remarks and references to Appendices
NONE BOSCH	3/2/18		Battalion less 2 Platoons at work on the Army Line, the 2 Hampshires have been withdrawn from the work. Two platoons of "D" Company engaged in the Construction of the Battle Track along the N. boundary of the Corps. Orders have been received that G.O.C. 30th Division will inspect the battalion tomorrow.	

Headquarters,
    30th. British Division. A.

    Attached please find the War Diary of the 6th. Bn. South Wales Borderers (Pioneers) for the Month of August 1918.

3/9/18.

                                    Alfred Kellett   Major for
            O.C., 6th. Bn. So. Wales Borderers (Pioneers).

WO 35

Army Form C. 2118.

WAR DIARY
or
INTELLIGENCE SUMMARY. 6TH Bn. SOUTH WALES BORDERERS.

(Erase heading not required.)

Instructions regarding War Diaries and Intelligence Summaries are contained in F. S. Regs., Part II. and the Staff Manual respectively. Title pages will be prepared in manuscript.

Place	Date	Hour	Summary of Events and Information	Remarks and references to Appendices
NONE BOSCH	1/8/18		"D" Coy had details proceeded to work on TRACKS leading to and from the Army Line	J.F.S.
do	2/8/18		"D" Company has details carried out the same work as yesterday. Lewis Gun training for N.C.O's under supervision of Lewis Gun officer	J.F.S.
do	3/8/18		Lewis Gun training was carried out under the supervision of the Lewis Gun Officer. "A" "B" Companies and 2 Platoons of "D" Coy proceeded to work on the Army Line at 8am. The remaining two Platoons of "D" Coy remained in Camp for baths and to carry out practice on the range	J.F.S.
do	4/8/18		Parties from "D" and "H.Q" Companies attended Church Service at 8½ Bdye H.Q. A party consisting of 2/Lt. Murston and 7 O.R. from "A" Coy attended the Butts at the Army Church Parade Service. "A" and "B" Companies carried out practice on the range.	J.F.S.
do	5/8/18		The Batt. (less "D" Coy) moved by march route to OXELAERE at 2 p.m. (Route: - via STEENVOORDE and CASSEL) "D" Coy proceeded to work on the Army Line at 6 a.m. returning at 12 noon	J.F.S.

WAR DIARY
or
INTELLIGENCE SUMMARY.
(Erase heading not required.)

Army Form C. 2118.

Place	Date	Hour	Summary of Events and Information	Remarks and references to Appendices
OXELAERE	6/8/18		Training was carried out by the Coys during the day. H.M. THE KING passed by about 10.30 a.m. "D" Coy rejoined the Batt. during the afternoon	JFS.
do	7/8/18		Major Reid-Kellett M.C. lectured all subaltern officers in the afternoon. Parties of A, B, & D Companies attended a Gas Demonstration at St Sylvestre Cappell. The remainder carried out training as usual	JFS.
do	8/8/18		Warning order received to be prepared to move to the forward area. During the day the Coys had baths, and then carried out the usual training. Lewis Gun Teams trained under the supervision of the Lewis Gun Officer. The Transport Officer proceeded to reconnoitre a position for Batt. Transport Lines in the forward area.	JFS.
do	9/8/18		The Batt. moved by march route, from Oxelaere, via Cassel, Steenvoorde, None Bosch, Godewaersvelde, Boeschepe to R.11b - R.12a, at 9.30 a.m. A halt was made at NONE. BOSCH for the purpose of serving dinner and the Batt. eventually arrived in the new area about 6 p.m.	JFS.

Army Form C. 2118.

WAR DIARY
or
INTELLIGENCE SUMMARY.
(Erase heading not required.)

Instructions regarding War Diaries and Intelligence Summaries are contained in F.S. Regs., Part II. and the Staff Manual respectively. Title pages will be prepared in manuscript.

Place	Date	Hour	Summary of Events and Information	Remarks and references to Appendices
do.	9/8/18		Major Reed-Kellett M.C. remained at Transport Lines; supervising the training of the Instructional Platoon.	J.F.S.
WESTOUTRE AREA	10/8/18		"A" Company commenced work on the roads, "C" and "D" Coys commenced work on the communication Trenches. The work by the latter Coys had to be carried out by night	J.F.S.
do	11/8/18		Work carried out as yesterday	J.F.S.
do.	12/8/18		To-day "C" Coy commenced work on the Left Sub-sector (21st Inf Bde) area. "D" Coy carried on similar work on the right sub-sector (89th Inf Bde area)	J.F.S.
do	13/8/18		Work carried out as yesterday	J.F.S
do	14/8/18		Work as usual.	J.F.S
do	15/8/18		Work as usual.	J.F.S

Army Form C. 2118.

WAR DIARY
or
INTELLIGENCE SUMMARY.

(Erase heading not required.)

Instructions regarding War Diaries and Intelligence Summaries are contained in F.S. Regs., Part II. and the Staff Manual respectively. Title pages will be prepared in manuscript.

Place	Date	Hour	Summary of Events and Information	Remarks and references to Appendices
do	16/8/18		Commencing to-day "C" Coy was absorbed into half Coys for work. One half to work with the 21st Inf. Bdge. and the other half with the 90th Inf Bdge.	J.F.S.
do	17/8/18		C, "A", "D" and "C" Companies reconnoitred the centre, right and left Bdge areas respectively with a view to selecting places where their Coys could construct suitable habitations.	J.F.S.
do	18/8/18		The N.C.O's and men who attended a course of instruction with the "Instructional Platoon" during the past week, returned to their respective companies in the Forward Area. The N.C.O's and men detailed for the next course proceeded to the Transport Lines in the afternoon. During the morning and afternoon the Coys bathed near BORSCHEPE. In the evening "C" and "D" Companies moved to their new positions in the Forward Area. No work was carried out to-day	J.F.S.
do	19/8/18		"A" Coy commenced work on the centre Brigade C.T. A draft of 2 off and 130 O.R. joined the Batt. to-day.	J.F.S.

WAR DIARY
or
INTELLIGENCE SUMMARY.

(Erase heading not required.)

Army Form C. 2118.

Place	Date	Hour	Summary of Events and Information	Remarks and references to Appendices
WESTOUTRE AREA	20/8/18		Movement of "H.Q.", "C" and "D" Companies into their new positions was completed this morning. Orders were received that "B" Coy. would work on the BLUE LINE with 201st Fd. Coy. R.E. One Officer and 2 N.C.O's proceeded on a course at 10th Corps Anti Gas School.	J.F.S
do	23/8/18		Work was carried out as for yesterday. Commencing to-day the Batt. was distributed for work as follows. "A" Coy and 2 Platoons "C" Coy under C.R.E on roads and BLUE LINE. 2 Platoons "D" Coy under 89th Brigade. 2 " " 90th " 2 " "C" Coy " 21st Brigade	J.F.S
do	24/8/18		Four N.C.O's proceeded on a course of Signalling at 2nd Army School.	J.F.S
do	25/8/18		N.C.O's and men who attended this weeks course with the "Instructional Platoon", rejoined their Coys in the "Forward Area". Those for the next course proceeded to the Transport lines in the afternoon. One Officer and two N.C.O's proceeded on a course of instruction at Second Army Musketry School.	J.F.S

WAR DIARY or INTELLIGENCE SUMMARY.

(Erase heading not required.)

Army Form C. 2118.

Instructions regarding War Diaries and Intelligence Summaries are contained in F. S. Regs., Part II. and the Staff Manual respectively. Title pages will be prepared in manuscript.

Place	Date	Hour	Summary of Events and Information	Remarks and references to Appendices
WESTOUTRE AREA	26/8/18		Work carried out as usual	J.F.S.
do	27/8/18		Work as usual. A draft of four O.R. (bandsmen) arrived to-day	J.F.S.
do	28/8/18		A draft of 46 O.R. arrived to-day and proceeded to join their respective Companies in the forward area.	J.F.S.
do	29/8/18		Work carried out as usual.	J.F.S.
do	30/8/18		Three N.C.O's proceeded on a Course of Instruction at 10th Corps Anti-Gas School. One Officer and N.C.O. proceeded on a course at G.H.Q. Lewis Gun School, Le TOUQUET.	J.F.S.
do	31/8/18		One Officer and 8 O.R. proceeded to 2nd Army Rest Camp.	J.F.S.

W Crawford
Lt Col

REPORT ON OPERATIONS CARRIED OUT BY THE
6th (S). BATTALION, SOUTH WALES BORDERERS, (PIONEERS).,
on the night of the 22nd /23rd AUGUST 1918.

Two platoons of "C" Company again proceeded to the work which had been abandoned the night before and this was completed.

The remainder of the Company worked in SHRIMP ALLEY,

Casualties amounting to 3 O.Rs Killed and 3 O.Rs wounded. were sustained during the completion of this work.

"D" Company moved forward to the scene of the previous nights work and this also was completed, so that a complete belt of double apron wire had been erected along the whole front.

@@@

REPORT ON OPERATIONS CARRIED OUT BY THE
6th (S). BATTALION, SOUTH WALES BORDERERS, (PIONEERS).
On the night of the 21st/22nd AUGUST 1918.

"A" Company rested during the day and moved off again at 8.45 p.m. and on arriving at the "sunken road" M.28.a. the enemy suddenly opened a very heavy barrage, including a number of gas shells, to cover a counter-attack on the ground captured the previous morning, this lasted until 11.50 p.m. The Company then proceeded to the trench which they had already established the previous night and commenced to dig the traverses which they completed. At 4 a.m. the Company left off work and returned to camp. Casualties sustained were 2 O.Rs wounded.

The two platoons of "C" Company set out to complete the wiring which had to be left the previous night. Owing to the enemy opening out and a counter-attack this was not carried out.

The remaining two platoons worked on SHRIMP ALLEY and only 1 casualty was sustained.

"D" Company moved off at 9.30 p.m. to continue on the same work as the previous night, but owing to the heavy shelling (which unfortunately caused a great number of casualties) the work had to be abandoned until the following night.

REPORT ON OPERATIONS CARRIED OUT BY THE
6th (S). BATTALION, SOUTH WALES BORDERERS, (PIONEERS).
On the Night of 20/21st AUGUST 1918.

On the night of the 20/21st August the Battalion took part in a minor operation carried out ~~carried out~~ on DRANOUTRE RIDGE.

"A" Company were under the orders of the Commanding Officer of the 2/14th LONDON Regiment and were held responsible for siting a support trench immediately the objective had been reached.

By 1.30 a.m. (21st) this Company together with three Companies of the LONDON SCOTTISH Regiment had arrived at the assembly positions on the S.E. side of the LOCRE-BAILLEUL road.

At 2.5 a.m. our barrage opened and the troops moved forward, very little opposition was met and the enemy barrage did not come down until 2.15 a.m.

The objective was reached by 2.50 a.m. and a line of outposts established on the E. side of the LOCRE - DRANOUTRE road, the Company then commenced digging on a line running from M.29.c.7.9. to M.35.a.8.8. Work was continued until 5 a.m. when the Company withdrew to BENGER COPSE arriving there at 6.30 a.m. Only 4 casualties were sustained.

Two platoons of "C" Company under the command of 2/Lieut F. Ravenscroft were allotted the task of wiring our front line running from M.23.d.9.1. to M.29.b.5.6. This they succeeded in erecting except for a distance of 100 yards.
The remaining two platoons worked on SHRIMP ALLEY.
The casualties for this company amounted to 2 O.Rs wounded.

"D" Company were allotted the task of consolidating the support line by digging and wiring three strong points on the reverse slope of the ridge. By 1 a.m. (21st) the Company had assembled in the neighbourhood of CHATEAU RD ready to move forward directly the objective had been taken, owing to the fog the pre-arranged light signals were not vissible and definite information was not received until 4 a.m. Immediately on receipt of this news the Company moved forward and commenced work, but at daybreak they withdrew, (5.30 a.m.)

@@

Army Form C. 2118.

WAR DIARY
or
INTELLIGENCE SUMMARY

(Erase heading not required.) 6th. (S). BN. SOUTH WALES BORDERERS (PIONEERS).

Vol 36

Place	Date	Hour	Summary of Events and Information	Remarks and references to Appendices
WESTOUTRE	1/9/18		Lieut W.L. Bowen M.C. died of wounds, and 2/Lt Marton wounded. Lieut Dayton appointed Medical Officer of the Battalion during the absence of Capt. Maclean R.A.M.C.	F S
do	2/9/18		Major Pearson D.S.O. M.C. proceeded to command the 2/16 London Regt. Lieut A.G. Pearce took over command and payment of A. Coy.	F S
do	3/9/18		The Battalion moved into a position on the LOCRE - BAILLEUL road and were joined by Advanced Batt. Headquarters on the same day.	F S
LOCRE	4/9/18		Two platoons of "A" Coy were attached to R.F.A. forward The remaining two platoons continued to erect Coy shelters. C and D Coys during the day erected shelters for their own use.	F S
do	5/9/18		Companies carried on with work as per programme Batt: Headquarters established at Sh. a.8.2. Sheet 28.	F S

Army Form C. 2118.

WAR DIARY
or
INTELLIGENCE SUMMARY.
(Erase heading not required.)

Instructions regarding War Diaries and Intelligence Summaries are contained in F. S. Regs., Part II. and the Staff Manual respectively. Title pages will be prepared in manuscript.

Place	Date	Hour	Summary of Events and Information	Remarks and references to Appendices
LOCRE	6/9/18		Capt Owen M.C. and 2 Sergts. proceeded to attend a Pioneer Course assembling on the 7th at Roam. During the day baths were arranged for the various Platoons not on work, and afterwards Kit inspection and drill were carried out. A draft of 8 O.R. joined the Battalion	JFS
do	7/9/18		Capt Davies T.H. took over command and payment of "A" Coy from Lt A.E. Pearce. M.C. Lt A.E. Pearce M.C. took over command and payment of "C" Coy from 2Lt. Shearing. The remainder of "C" and "D" Coys bathed during the day. The two Platoons of "D" Coy attached to 89th Brigade were relieved during the day.	JFS
do	8/9/18		The Batt. less "D" Coy and two Platoons of "A" Coy moved forward to a new area in the vicinity of KEMMEL HILL. Transport and	

WAR DIARY
or
INTELLIGENCE SUMMARY.

(Erase heading not required.)

Army Form C. 2118.

Instructions regarding War Diaries and Intelligence Summaries are contained in F. S. Regs., Part II. and the Staff Manual respectively. Title pages will be prepared in manuscript.

Place	Date	Hour	Summary of Events and Information	Remarks and references to Appendices
do	8/9/18		Quartermaster's stores remained at the original location. One platoon of "B" Coy were placed at disposal of C.B. Headquarters. Coy turned Sheltus. The remainder of "B" Coy commenced to work on the repair of the track from GORDON RD to the new Batt. Headquarters.	J.F.S.
KEMMEL	9/9/18		Lt Griffiths having reported for duty was posted to "D" Coy. Coy's spent the day in improving the Camp.	J.F.S.
do	10/9/18		"D" Coy moved to the vicinity of Batt Headquarters. One platoon of "A" Coy worked on the repair of the DAYLIGHT CORNER — NEUVE EGLISE road, whilst the remaining Platoon worked on the WULVERGHEM — NEUVE EGLISE road. "C" Coy worked on the clearing and repairing of the GORDON ROAD	J.F.S.

Army Form C. 2118.

WAR DIARY
or
INTELLIGENCE SUMMARY.
(Erase heading not required.)

Instructions regarding War Diaries and Intelligence Summaries are contained in F. S. Regs., Part II. and the Staff Manual respectively. Title pages will be prepared in manuscript.

Place	Date	Hour	Summary of Events and Information	Remarks and references to Appendices
KEMMEL	11/9/18		A draft of 12 N.C.O's and men reported at the Battalion today	JFS
			Work was carried out as for yesterday	JFS
do	12/9/18		"A" Coy continued the work on the road through WULVERGHEM village	
			"C" Coy worked on WULVERGHEM - RE FARM road, and also on the LOCRE road	JFS
			"D" Coy worked as detailed by 89th Inf Brigade	
do	13/9/18		Work carried out as for yesterday	JFS
do	14/9/18		Lieut Kendrick and 12 O.R. proceeded to 2nd Army Rest Camp.	
			Work as for yesterday. Three O.R. proceeded to attend a Course of Instruction at the 10th Corps School.	JFS

WAR DIARY
or
INTELLIGENCE SUMMARY.

(Erase heading not required.)

Army Form C. 2118.

Place	Date	Hour	Summary of Events and Information	Remarks and references to Appendices
KEMMEL	15/9/18		Work was carried out as detailed verbally by the Commanding Officer.	JFS
do	16/9/18		Two Platoons "A" Coy worked on repair of track from GORDON ROAD to Batt Headquarters. "C" Company repaired the DRANOUTRE – SWINDON road. Five O.R. reported back from hospital	JFS
do	17/9/18		Capt Cox M. and Lieut Jones R.A.C. having reported for duty took over the Command and fragment of "A" and "C" Coys respectively. "A" and "C" Coys carried out escort as for yesterday, and "D" Coy as per orders received from Brigade	JFS
do	18/9/18		Two platoons of "A" Coy returned the Coy from Bdges of R.F.A. to which they have been attached. Two platoons "A" Coy worked on the DRANOUTRE – SWINDON road.	JFS

Army Form C. 2118.

WAR DIARY
or
INTELLIGENCE SUMMARY.
(Erase heading not required.)

Instructions regarding War Diaries and Intelligence Summaries are contained in F.S. Regs., Part II. and the Staff Manual respectively. Title pages will be prepared in manuscript.

Place	Date	Hour	Summary of Events and Information	Remarks and references to Appendices
KEMMEL	18/9/18		"C" Coy carried out work under an R.E. officer on the truck south of WULVERGHEM. "D" Coy worked as per Brigade Orders.	JFS
do	19/9/18		One platoon "A" Coy worked on clearing House standing and collecting timber for same. The remaining three platoons worked on the DRANOUTRE-SWINDON road. "C" Coy carried out work as for yesterday and "D" Coy worked as per Brigade orders	JFS
do	20/9/18		Work carried out as for yesterday	JFS
do	21/9/18		"A" Coy moved into new area at S.18.a.3.7. All details at the Transport lines resumed their respective jobs to-day	JFS

Army Form C. 2118.

WAR DIARY
or
INTELLIGENCE SUMMARY.
(Erase heading not required.)

Instructions regarding War Diaries and Intelligence Summaries are contained in F. S. Regs, Part II. and the Staff Manual respectively. Title pages will be prepared in manuscript.

Place	Date	Hour	Summary of Events and Information	Remarks and references to Appendices
KEMMEL	22/9/18		2/Lieut Chappell and 3 N.C.O's proceeded to attend an Anti Gas Course assembling at the 10th Corps School. Work as for yesterday	JFS
do	23/9/18		Two officers and five O.R. joined the Battalion. Work was carried out as for yesterday	JFS.
do	24/9/18		During the day Headquarter Coy bathed	JFS
	25/9/18		Work was carried out as arranged. One Coy took proceeded on a Course of Instruction in Cookery assembling at LUMBRES.	JFS
	26/9/18		"C" Coy remained in Camp for baths and inspection. The remaining two Coys carried out work as usual. Battalion Serjeant Major reported for Duty. (RSM Reason)	JFS

Army Form C. 2118.

WAR DIARY
or
INTELLIGENCE SUMMARY.
(Erase heading not required.)

Instructions regarding War Diaries and Intelligence Summaries are contained in F.S. Regs., Part II. and the Staff Manual respectively. Title pages will be prepared in manuscript.

Place	Date	Hour	Summary of Events and Information	Remarks and references to Appendices
KEMMEL Hut	27/9/18	—	One officer (2Lt G Sanchard) & other ranks proceeded to Brn Army Rest Camp at AUDRESSELLES. 2Lt Grigor, & other ranks proceeded to X Corps Gas School. Companies stood by awaiting orders.	
do	28/9/18	—	All companies paraded for work at 4.30 am. A+T Companies working on repair of Wulverghem - MESSINES Rd. "D" Company working on WULVERGHEM - WYTSCHAETE Rd, - WULVERGHEM - LA PLUS DOUVE FARM - GOOSEBERRY FARM Rd. and bridging. Jot meals were taken up to Companies on the work.	
do	30/9/18	—	2 Companies were employed on renewing fill trees and accommodation in the new forward area. 1 Company employed on WULVERGHEM - WYTSCHAETE Rd by KRUISSTRAAT CRATERS and WULVERGHEM - LA PLUS DOUVE Fm - GOOSEBERRY FARM Rd.	

(A9475) Wt W2358/P36 600,000 12/17 D. D. & L. Sch. 82a. Forms/C118/15.

CONFIDENTIAL

Headquarters,
   30th. British Division.   "A".

Herewith War Diary of 6th.(S).Bn. The South Wales Borderers (Pioneers) for the month of October 1918.

Please acknowledge.

                                                  Major,
5/11/18.   Commdg. 6th. Bn. S.W. Borderers (Pnrs:).

ORIGINAL.
Army Form C. 2118.

6th. (S.) Bn. SOUTH WALES BORDERERS (PION B RRS)
WAR DIARY
or
INTELLIGENCE SUMMARY.
(Erase heading not required.)

Instructions regarding War Diaries and Intelligence Summaries are contained in F. S. Regs., Part II. and the Staff Manual respectively. Title pages will be prepared in manuscript.

Place	Date	Hour	Summary of Events and Information	Remarks and references to Appendices
Fides	Oct 1		Lt RJ Griffith with 2 ors proceeded to Lewis Gun Course at F Corps School	
"	2		Battalion continued work on repair of road in the neighbourhood of WYTSCHAETE – OOSTAVERNE – HOUTHEM One company (C) working under orders of 9th Inf Brigade	
"	3		Road work in the same area continued	
"	4		Battalion repairing roads. Lt J Teague MC & 2 sergeants proceeded to Pioneer Course at ROUEN	
"	5		Battalion rested. Chapel hrs carried out. Capt JC Owen MC rejoined from Pioneer Course ROUEN	
"	6		"A" & "C" Companies working with 201 & 202 Field Cops RE on Klein road (P.13.c)	

WAR DIARY
or
INTELLIGENCE SUMMARY.

Army Form C. 2118.

(Erase heading not required.)

Place	Date	Hour	Summary of Events and Information	Remarks and references to Appendices
July	7		A & C Companies continued work on plank road P.13.c. 1 Aug working on repair roads in neighbourhood of TENBRIELEN 2. Sappers proceeded to Signaling Course at VII Corps School. D Company moved under Company arrangements to an area forward of HOUTHEM	
"	8.		The Battalion continued work as for the 7th inst	
"	9.		Work on plank road continued. also repair roads around TENBRIELEN	
"	10.		All companies working on plank road. 2.OR reported for duty. taken on strength	
"	11		Work as for yesterday. Roads repaired neighbourhood of TENBRIELEN — AMERICA — HOUTHEM 2/Lt Smith & 3 OR proceeded to X Corps Gas School 8. OR proceeded to 2nd Army Rest Camp AUDRESSELLES	

WAR DIARY
or
INTELLIGENCE SUMMARY.

Army Form C. 2118.

Place	Date	Hour	Summary of Events and Information	Remarks and references to Appendices
Field	11th		The names of the W/m NCOs & men brought forward to notice for acts of gallantry.	
			H/Qrs CSM. Green J. M.M.	
			6/13670 Sgt. Evans A.J. M.M.	
			16428 A/C Rees J.	
"	12th		Coys the Battalion working on opening up & repairing roads in the neighbourhood of IENBRIELEN – WERVICQ – BLOKSTRAAT – EAST – AMERICA CRST. – KRISTMOLEN. "J" day. A/C Rees J. Transport awarded the Military Medal.	
"	13th		4 OR reported for duty & taken on strength. Battalion rested	
"	14th		A & C Companies working on Plank Road P.B.C. D Coy. clearing roads in & around HOUTHEM, working on Plank Roadwith "C" Company	

Army Form C. 2118.

WAR DIARY
or
INTELLIGENCE SUMMARY.
(Erase heading not required.)

Place	Date	Hour	Summary of Events and Information	Remarks and references to Appendices
July	15		"A" Company & H.Q Company moved forward to an area P.6.a. (AMERICA). "C" Coy working on Plank Road P.13.c. "D" Company repairing roads neighbourhood of AMERICA EAST towards MENIN	
"	16		"A" Company working on repair of roads around KRUISTOKEN Capt W Davies took on command & payment of D Coy. Battalion moved to AMERICA	
"	17		Battalion moved forward to COUCOU near MENIN	
"	18		A & C Companies preparing approaches to bridge at R.19.c.1.9. "D" Coy employed on repairing roads in CouCou working south E. Coy.	
"	19		A & C companies working on road approach to bridge as per yesterday. "D" Company working on roads in BOUSBECQUE	

WAR DIARY
or
INTELLIGENCE SUMMARY.

(Erase heading not required.)

Army Form C. 2118.

Place	Date	Hour	Summary of Events and Information	Remarks and references to Appendices
Delhi	July 19		6/1367 Sergt. Evans AJ awarded Bar to M.M.	
			3 O.R. reported for duty & taken on strength	
	20.		C & D Companies working on approach to bridge	
			R19.C.1.9. "A" Company holed	
			2/Lt Griffith R. took over duties of Transport Officer	
			less C. Coy	
	21.		Battalion moved to ROLLEGHEM. "C" Company remained	
			at COUCOU.	
	22		Battalion moved to St GENOIS 15 Casualties	
			sustained during the night	
	23		Battalion moved back to an area U.7.a..	
	24.		A & D Companies occupied on repair of forward	
			roads about St. GENOIS — DRIES — COYGHEM	

WAR DIARY
or
INTELLIGENCE SUMMARY.

(Erase heading not required.)

Army Form C. 2118.

Place	Date	Hour	Summary of Events and Information	Remarks and references to Appendices
Reld	25th		A + D Companies continued work repairing road. 6 O.R. proceeded to X Corps Reinforcement Platoon. Numerous O.R. evacuated to Field Ambulance owing to Influenza	
"	26.		Plank for Plank Road at HERCHIN carried to JEICHM from COUGHEM. A+D Coys providing loading parties.	
"	27.		A+D Companies working on repair of roads in COUGHEM- DRIES	
-	28.		"D" Company working on plank road & bridge at LOCK-NO 5. Also provided loading & timber cutting parties. "A" Coy. work on repair of roads.	

C. 2118.
Army Form C. 2118.

WAR DIARY
or
INTELLIGENCE SUMMARY.
(Erase heading not required.)

Instructions regarding War Diaries and Intelligence Summaries are contained in F. S. Regs., Part II. and the Staff Manual respectively. Title pages will be prepared in manuscript.

Place	Date	Hour	Summary of Events and Information	Remarks and references to Appendices
Field	29		"A" D Companies continued work on approach to bridge at Lock no 5.	
"	30		Batt. Headquarters moved to U.1.6.4.5. Road Repairs continued. Site for new bridge at Moen reconnoitred & approaches to same levelled. "C" Company rejoined from detachment at Menin	
"	31		Work on approaches to bridge at Moen continued. Major D.H. Shekle be assumed Temporary Command of the Battalion Lt Col Cranford D.S.O. proceeded leave to UK 27/8 to 16/18	

LM Shekle Major,
Commdg. 6th. (S). Bn. S. W. Borderers (Pnrs).

CONFIDENTIAL.

30th Division No. A/9569

D.A.G., B A S E.

With reference to this Office A/9481 dated 14.12.1918, herewith War Diary of the 6th Bn. South Wales Borderers for the month of November, 1918.

Brigadier General.
Commanding 30th British Division.

16.12.1918.

Confidential
War Cabinet.
Memorandum for
November 1918
of British and
French Commanders.

9243
30

H.O.S.
10pp

ORIGINAL

Army Form C. 2118.

WAR DIARY
INTELLIGENCE SUMMARY

6th (S.) Bn. South Wales Borderers (Pioneers)

(Erase heading not required.)

Place	Date	Hour	Summary of Events and Information	Remarks and references to Appendices
FARM 2000x N.E. of SAINT-GENOIS.	1/11/18		The Battalion engaged preparing material and approaches for new bridges, repairing roads, and filling craters etc.	R.
do	2/11/18		The Battalion worked on roads near SAINT-GENOIS crater filling etc and on roads near DRIES.	R.
do	3/11/18		"A" Coy employed cleaning up, kit inspections etc. "D" Coy work on plank road commencing at 0800 hrs and were relieved by "C" Coy at 14.00 hrs. This Coy carried on till 20.00 hrs.	R.
			AWARDS	
			Under authority granted by His Majesty the King, the Field Marshal Commanding-in-Chief, has been pleased to grant the following award to the undermentioned Warrant-Officer.	
			THE DISTINGUISHED CONDUCT MEDAL	
			No 46495 C.S.M. T. GREEN "C" Coy.	
			The Army Corps and Divisional Commanders congratulate the recipient. (Authority MS./H/11477 dated 30/10/18	R.

WAR DIARY
or
INTELLIGENCE SUMMARY.

Army Form C. 2118.

(Erase heading not required.)

Place	Date	Hour	Summary of Events and Information	Remarks and references to Appendices
FARMS NEAR SAINT-GENOIS	4/11/18		"A" Coy. were engaged filling in a crater at level crossing 1500x NE of MOEN. "B" Coy engaged filling roads through MOEN in a state of repair. "D" Coy arranged baths and held inspection. Casualties to "A" Coy. 6 other Ranks wounded.	R. R. R.
do	5/11/18		Bn engaged keeping roads in repair in the vicinity of SAINT-GENOIS, MOEN, BOSSUYT, AVELGHEM.	R.
do	6/11/18		The Bn moved by march route to an area about halfway between KNOKKE and MOEN	R. R.
KNOKKE	7/11/18		"A" "C" "D" Coys. moved HEESTERT. "A" & "D" Coys carry on with work on crater at junction of roads leading from AUTRYVE - AVELGHEM and ESCANAFFLES - AVELGHEM commencing work at 1500 hrs. "C" Coy worked on roads near ONKERDRIESCH and WOFFELSTRAAT also near RAAPTORE	R.

WAR DIARY
or
INTELLIGENCE SUMMARY.

(Erase heading not required.)

Army Form C. 2118.

Instructions regarding War Diaries and Intelligence
Summaries are contained in F.S. Regs., Part II.
and the Staff Manual respectively. Title pages
will be prepared in manuscript.

Place	Date	Hour	Summary of Events and Information	Remarks and references to Appendices
IPNORRE	6/11/18		"C" Coy carry on with work on roads. One party commencing at 14.00 hrs. and one at 16.00 hrs. "A" & "D" Coy. carry on with work on craters as for yesterday 5th inst.	
			POSTING.	
			MAJOR A.J. ELLIS having this day reported for duty is taken on the strength and will take over temporarily the duties of 2ND in Command.	
			COMMAND	
			Capt. R.M. COX M.C. will take over the command and payment of "A" Coy from 2/Lt A.E. KING as from today.	
			Capt. J.C. OWEN M.C. having reported this day for duty from hospital takes over the command and payment of "B" Coy from 2/Lt. A.J. Smith as from today.	R.
do.	7/11/18		Coy. work as on the 8th inst.	R.

Army Form C. 2118.

WAR DIARY
or
INTELLIGENCE SUMMARY.
(Erase heading not required.)

Instructions regarding War Diaries and Intelligence Summaries are contained in F. S. Regs., Part II. and the Staff Manual respectively. Title pages will be prepared in manuscript.

Place	Date	Hour	Summary of Events and Information	Remarks and references to Appendices
YNOKE	9/11/18		STRENGTH INCREASE	
			The 7/12 O.R. having reported today are taken on the strength and posted to companies as under:—	
			To "A" Coy — 9.	
			To "D" Coy — 8.	
			Casualties reported. "C" Coy — 1	
			"D" Coy — 1	R.
"	10/11/18		The Bn. moved by march route to AVELGHEM.	
			"C" Coy. employed making diversions, also A's D Coys. at junction of roads as far 4th inst.	R.
AVELGHEM	11/11/18		The Bn. moved by march route to AMOUGIES	R.
AMOUGIES	12/11/18		The Bn. moved by march route to WATRIPONT	R.
			A's D Coys. returning to billets in the vicinity of ANSŒROEL,	R.
WATRIPONT	13/11/18		Bn. Hd. Qrs. moves by march route to ANSŒROEL,	R.

Army Form C. 2118.

WAR DIARY
or
INTELLIGENCE SUMMARY.
(Erase heading not required.)

Instructions regarding War Diaries and Intelligence Summaries are contained in F. S. Regs., Part II. and the Staff Manual respectively. Title pages will be prepared in manuscript.

Place	Date	Hour	Summary of Events and Information	Remarks and references to Appendices
ANSEROEL	13/11/18		Coys. are employed repairing the ESCANAFFLES - RENAIX road.	R.
do.	14/11/18		Bn. work as for yesterday.	R.
do.	15/11/18		Bn. work as for yesterday.	R.
do.	16/11/18		Bn. work as on 15 inst. One other rank rejoined from Base Depot.	R.
do.	17/11/18		and posted to "D" Coy. The Bn. moved by march route to HEESTERT	R.
HEESTERT AELBEKE	18/11/18		The Bn. moved by march route to AELBEKE	R.
do.	19/11/18		The Bn. was employed cleaning up and holding inspections	R.
do.	20/11/18		The Bn. Cony. on 10th Infantry Training 09-00 hrs. to 12-30 hrs. The afternoon being devoted to recreational training.	R.
			COMMAND Lt. Col. W.L. CRAWFORD. D.S.O. having returned from leave takes over the command of the Bn. from Maj. D.H. STICKLER M.C. (Maj. D.H. STICKLER M.C.)	
			STRENGTH.	
do.			The 7 other ranks joined from Base Depot- on the 15th inst- and	R.

WAR DIARY
or
INTELLIGENCE SUMMARY.
(Erase heading not required.)

Army Form C. 2118.

Place	Date	Hour	Summary of Events and Information	Remarks and references to Appendices
AELBEKE	20/11/18		and are posted to Coys. as under:-	
			"A" Coy. - 16.	
			"C" Coy. - 7	
			"D" Coy. - 9	R.
do	21/11/18		Training. Companies carried out training as per programme rendered to the Bn. Orderly Room today	R.
do	22/11/18		Bn. Parade at 09.15 hrs. Training. Companies, after Battalion Parade will march off and continue their training as per programme. Educational Classes were held from 4.30 PM till 6.30 PM	R.
do	23/11/18		Companies continue with training as per Programme. Afternoon devoted to Sports. Educational Classes from 4.30 PM till 6.30 PM for French (Elementary)	

Army Form C. 2118.

WAR DIARY
or
INTELLIGENCE SUMMARY.
(Erase heading not required.)

Instructions regarding War Diaries and Intelligence Summaries are contained in F. S. Regs., Part II. and the Staff Manual respectively. Title pages will be prepared in manuscript.

Place	Date	Hour	Summary of Events and Information	Remarks and references to Appendices
AELBEKE	23/1/18		Shorthand, First-Aid, Arithmetic (Elementary)	R.
do.	24/1/18		Church Parade for C. of E. at 10.00 hrs. Roman Catholics at 09.45 hrs.	R.
			COMMAND MAJ. A.J. ELLIS. takes over the duties of Second-in-Command from MAJ. D.H. STICKLER. M.C as from today.	
			MAJ. D.H. STICKLER. takes over the command of 'D' Coy. from CAPT. T.H. DAVIES, as from today.	
do	25/1/18		EDUCATION: Examinations of companies were held for Classification of Education.	R.
do	26/1/18		The Bn. paraded for route march at 09.00 hrs. Distance 9 miles. Educational Classes were held at 16.00 hrs.	R. R.
do	27/1/18		STRENGTH One O.R. reported from BASE DEPOT and posted to 'A' Coy.	R.
			Commanding Officers' Inspection at 09.10 hrs. held as per Programme.	R. R.

Army Form C. 2118.

WAR DIARY
or
INTELLIGENCE SUMMARY.
(Erase heading not required.)

Place	Date	Hour	Summary of Events and Information	Remarks and references to Appendices
AELBEKE	28/11/18		Battalion Parade at 09.16 hr. for C.O.s Inspection afterwards Companies Parade to train as per programme	R.
do	29/11/18		Battalion Parade 09.00 hrs Companies train as per programme.	R.
do	30/11/18		Bn. moved by march route to LINSELLES	R.

W Crawford, Lieut Col.
Comdg. 6th 13n. De Wake Borderers (Canr)

Rec'd
9/R 44

War Diary
of South Wales Borderers
for
December 1918

Army Form C. 2118.

WAR DIARY
or
INTELLIGENCE SUMMARY.
(Erase heading not required.)

6/S.W. Borderers.

Instructions regarding War Diaries and Intelligence Summaries are contained in F. S. Regs., Part II. and the Staff Manual respectively. Title pages will be prepared in manuscript.

Place	Date	Hour	Summary of Events and Information	Remarks and references to Appendices
LINSELLES	December 1918 1	09.20	Battalion continued march. Route QUESNOY – CROIX-AU-BOIS – FONQUEREAU.	A/S.
FONQUEREAU	2	09.10	Battalion continued march. Route LA PREVOTE – FREELINGHEM Road – HOURLINES Road – ARMENTIERES – ERQUINGHEM.	
			SAILLEY-SUR-LA LYS – ESTAIRES – LA GORGUE.	A/S.
LA GORGUE	3	09.22	Battalion continued march. Route Junction South of MERVILLE Station – CALONNE-SUR-LYS – ST. FLORIS – ST. VENANT.	A/S.
ST. VENANT	4	09.30	Battalion continued march. Route HAVERSKERQUE – STEENBECQUE – SERCUS – LYND E – EBBLINGHEM.	A/S.
EBBLINGHEM	5		Battalion settling into its billets and cleaning up. Companies scattered. 'D' Company billets bad.	A/S.
"	6		LIEUT. W.J. KENDRICK transferred from 'D' to 'A' Company. Inspection of Companies by C.O. Hill-inspection, P.T. and cleaning up of kit.	A/S.
"	7		C.O. inspected H.Q. and 'C' Coy. The CROIX DE GUERRE awarded to 6/17544 Cpl. W. BAYNES and 29782 Pte. W. DICKS.	
			The following officers were put in charge of games and sports. RUGBY FOOTBALL – CAPTAIN A.C. MANN, M.C. R.A.M.C.
			ASSOCIATION FOOTBALL – LIEUT. S. KELLY. ATHLETICS – LIEUT. S. KELLY. CINEMA and CONCERT PARTY – Rev. B.R. PARSLEW.
			C.F. BOXING – CAPTAIN L. PETTS. M.C. A reading and writing room was opened in the Boys School.	A/S.
"	8		Divine Service held on Company parade grounds. R.C's in Village Church. S.A.A. returned to BR.MR.STORE. 1 Casual report.	
			and posted to 'A' Coy. 4 Lt. Sgts. C.S.M. GREEN. T. 2 Sgts. and 2 Corporals proceeded to U.K.	A/S.
"	9		CAPTAIN T.H. DAVIES appointed Battalion Education Officer. Company found its sundry A.C. Corps.	A/S.
"	10		Corporal and 2 O/R sent to Corps Reception Camp for duty. 19 N.C.O's and O/R reported for duty.	A/S.
"	11		Companies found its Company and Command D.M. 14359 C.S.M.S. LARGE. T. and 29 N.C.O's and O/R demobilized.	A/S.

Army Form C. 2118.

WAR DIARY 6/S.W.Borders.
or
INTELLIGENCE SUMMARY.

(Erase heading not required.)

Instructions regarding War Diaries and Intelligence Summaries are contained in F. S. Regs., Part II. and the Staff Manual respectively. Title pages will be prepared in manuscript.

Place	Date	Hour	Summary of Events and Information	Remarks and references to Appendices
	December 1915			
EBBLINGHEM	12	09.45	Battalion Drill. 2 o/R demobilized.	A/2.
"	13	09.15	Battalion Drill. Skin inspection by M.O.	A/2.
"	14	10.30	Inspection by G.O.C. Division. Officers and men exhibited, presented with ribbons. 2nd Lieut. F.P. WATKINS left to conduct a draft to U.K.	A/2.
"	15		Divine Service on Company Parade grounds. 15 o/R demobilized.	A/2.
"	16		'A' Coy. at work at RENESCURE. 'D' Coy. erecting Nissen hut. 'C' Coy. Platoon and Company Drill. H.Q. Transport and C/by battn.	A/2.
			39n S/Lt R. Mvd. to STAGING CAMP, HAZEBROUCK for duty. 2n.39139 Sgt. EDWARDS. WH. transpd for D'ty to H.Q. for Cantion work. 73 N.C.O.s and o/R demobilized.	A/2.
"	17		'A' and 'D' Coys. continue work. 'C' Coy. Platoon and Company Drill. 10 N.C.O. and 5 o/R demobilized.	A/2.
"	18		Work continued. 2 officers and 180 o/R proceeded to DUNKERQUE for the day.	A/2.
"	19		'A' Coy. continued work. 'C' and 'D' Coys. began construction of new camp.	A/2.
"	20		Work continued. Skin inspection by M.O.	A/2.
"	21		Work continued. Lecture at ST. OMER by DR. VAUGHAN-CORNISH, F.R.G.S. on geographical results attained by completion of the War. 6 Officers attended.	A/2.
"	22		R.C. parade service in village church.	A/2.
"	23		Work continued.	A/2.

Army Form C. 2118.

WAR DIARY 6/J.W. Borderers.
or
INTELLIGENCE SUMMARY.
(Erase heading not required.)

Place	Date	Hour	Summary of Events and Information	Remarks and references to Appendices
EBBLINGHEM.	December 1918 24		"A" Company training. "C" and "D" Coys. work on new Camp. MAJOR A. REID-KELLE T.T.M.C. 2 on 6/1/25 Sgt PEARCE M.M. 3 on. 6/1/427 Pte. BEARD M.M. awarded French CROIX DE GUERRE for gallantry in action.	a/2.
"	25	13.00	Men had their Christmas dinners. R.C. Service in village Church.	a/2.
"	26		Organised games.	a/2.
"	27		Work on new camp continued. 2 O/R. reported for duty. 31 O/R. C.O's and O/R. demobilized.	a/2.
"	28		Company training and work continued. Skin inspection by M.O. Lecture to Batln. on "The 24th K.L. Regimental Band Fête" 10/R. demobilized.	a/2.
"	29	10.30	Parade service of C.of.E. in the School room.	a/2.
"	30		Company Parades under O.C. Coys.	a/2.
"	31	11.30	Battalion marched to ARQUES to entrain, remainder of day for DUNKIRK.	a/3.

W.Crawford
LT. COLONEL
COMMANDING 6th (S.R.) Bn. R.W. BORDERERS

Headquarters "A"
30th Division

Herewith War Diary of this unit
for the month of January 1919, please

31/1/19

T. Letts
Capt adj't

for OC 6th South Wales Borderers. (B

P/30
6 SWB
9/82 45

Army Form C. 2118.

WAR DIARY
or
INTELLIGENCE SUMMARY.
(Erase heading not required.)

Instructions regarding War Diaries and Intelligence Summaries are contained in F.S. Regs., Part II. and the Staff Manual respectively. Title pages will be prepared in manuscript.

Place	Date	Hour	Summary of Events and Information	Remarks and references to Appendices
Dunkirk	January 1919 1	08.00	Detrained and marched to No. 6 camp MARDYKE. Batts. under canvas.	A/E
"	2		Camp improvement.	A/E
"	3		A, C and D Coys on work at HOSPICE camp.	A/E
"	4		A Coy work in MARDYK camp, C Coy and D Coy two 17ft and 25 men to continue work at HOSPICE camp. 10ft 25 men D Coy to work in MARDYK	
"	5		Camp 2 o/r demobilized.	A/E
"	6		Work as for 4th. 6 O/R demobilized.	A/E
"	7		A Coy same work. Segregated amm B Coy work in own camp for Batt. C Coy and remainder of D Coy as usual work.	A/E
"	8		A & C Coy usual work. 20 men of D Coy working with 201st Coy R.E. on Nissen huts in camp. Remainder of Coy on HOSPICE camp.	A/E
"	9		Coy. usual work. General education classes in the evening.	A/E
"	10	08.00	Work as for the 4th.	A/E
"	11		Batt. moved into areas Camps 8 O/R demobilized.	A/E
"	12	11.30	Coy work in camp and on their usual work. 13 O/R demobilized. Parade service in Cinema hut. Lieut. S. RELLY and 10/29 O/R. Page A. receive Belgium Croix de guerre. Capt. D. STICKLER, M.E. and Capt. T. H. DAVIES and 10 O/R demobilized.	A/E
"	13		Work as on Saturday. C Coy and H.R. battal.	A/E
"	14		A & C Coy usual work. D Coy battal.	A/E

Army Form C. 2118.

WAR DIARY
or
INTELLIGENCE SUMMARY.

(Erase heading not required.)

Instructions regarding War Diaries and Intelligence Summaries are contained in F. S. Regs., Part II. and the Staff Manual respectively. Title pages will be prepared in manuscript.

Place	Date	Hour	Summary of Events and Information	Remarks and references to Appendices
DUNKIRK.	January 1919 15		Coy. battal. c+D Coy. usual work. 17 O/R demobilized.	A/S.
"	16		Coy. on usual work. Half Transport personnel batted. 8 O/R demobilized.	A/S.
"	17		Coy. usual work. Half Transport personnel batted. Canteen Committee formed. 13 O/R demobilized.	A/S.
"	18		Coy. usual work. 4 O/R demobilized.	A/S.
"	19	10.30	Church Parade.	A/S.
"	20		Coy. usual work. Lecture by Lieut. S. KELLY on Demobilization in the evening.	A/S.
"	21		Coy. usual work. Educational classes in evening. 11 O/R demobilized.	A/S.
"	22		Coy. usual work. Lecture by the M.O. in the evening. 8 O/R demobilized.	A/S.
"	23		Coy. usual work. The following Officers and O/R were mentioned in despatches dated 8/11/18. Lieut.Col. L.C.W. DEANE. D.S.O.M.C. MAJOR N.G. PEARSON. M.S., MAJOR ARGIO-WELLETT.M.C. Capt. D.H. STICKLER M.C. Alcapt. S.E. RUMSEY. M.C. LIEUT. S. KELLY. No.1792 L/c. MEREDITH.G., No.2222 Pte. THOMAS. G. T., 9 O/R demobilized.	A/S.
"	24		Coy. usual work. No.17302 C.Q.M.S. EWING, D.A. No.28804 Sgt. EVANS. T. No.39665 Cpl. SUTAIN. W. awarded M.S.M. 8 O/R demobilized.	A/S.
"	25		Coy. usual work. C Coy. batted. No.15697 Sgt. HITCHINGS. J.F. awarded M.S.M. LIEUT.S.K.ELLY. No.15849 R.S.M. PEARSON P.J. and 11 O/R demobilized.	A/S.
"	26	9.20	Commemorative Parade Service. 10 O/R demobilized.	A/S.
"	27		Coy. usual work.	

Army Form C. 2118.

WAR DIARY
or
INTELLIGENCE SUMMARY. a/y.3.
(Erase heading not required.)

Place	Date	Hour	Summary of Events and Information	Remarks and references to Appendices
DUNKIRK.	January 1919 28		Coy. usual work. 8 o/R. demobilized.	a/y.3.
"	29		Coy. usual work. 8 o/R. demobilized.	a/y.3.
"	30		Coy. usual work. A Coy. bathed. 8 o/R demobilized.	a/y.3.
"	31		Coy. usual work. 2nd Lieut. R. GRIFFITHS took over duties of Transport-Officer from 2nd Lieut. F. RAVENSCROFT. No. 27623 Cpl. (A/Sgt.) ALLEN.C.H. 19764 Cpl. EDWARDS.J. 45695 Pte. PAYE.G. awarded M.M. for gallantry and devotion to duty. D Coy. bathed. 11 o/R demobilized.	a/y.3.

WAR DIARY
INTELLIGENCE SUMMARY
(Erase heading not required.)

Army Form C. 2118.

6 SWB
App 46

Place	Date	Hour	Summary of Events and Information	Remarks and references to Appendices
DUNKIRK	1 Decem 1918	10.00	Church Parade.	...
	2		Coys usual work. 7 o.r. demobilised	...
	3		A.C.& B Coys on works in Hospital Camp. 8 o.r. demobilised	...
	4		Coys work as for 3rd inst. 9 o.r. demobilised	...
	5		Coys usual work. 1 W.O. C.S.M.2 and 9 o.r. demobilised	...
	6		A.C.&.D. Coys under Lt. W.J. Kendrick to R.S. Fusiliers for work. 9 o.r. demobilised	...
	7		Work as for 6th. The following officers from 5th S.W.B. posted. Major J.T. Evans D.S.O. M.C. Lt. C.W. Capener. A 2/Lt. J.T. Williams "A". 7/Lt. A. Roberts "D". 2/Lt. P.C. Hull "D". 7/Lt. J.C. Boyd Jr. "D"	...
	8		Capt. R.S. Griffiths "C". 11 o.r. demobilised. 200 o.r. from 5th S.W.B. posted	...
	9	10.00	Church Parade. 12 o.r. demobilised	...
	10		A.&.O Coys work at Hospital Camp. C.i.C. in Camp.	...
			Major A.F. Ellis took over Command of Bn. Capt. R.S. Lewis 2nd in Command. Capt. R.S. Griffiths M.C. to be O.C. B Cy. Capt. J.C. Owen M.C. to Command "C" Cy. Capt. J.R.W. Jones M.C. to Command "A" Cy. 2/Lt. E. Chappel takes over T/QMR. 1 W.O. 11 o.r. demobilised	...
	11		A.&.C. Coys Missile Huts Hospital. "B" Coy in Camp. 2/Lt. O. Heast M.C. reported from 5th S.W.B.	...
	12		Coys usual work. Capt. J.C. Owen M.C. takes over 2/ic in Command. 5 J.O.R. demobilised	...
	13		Coys usual work. 2/Lt. R. Grigsby takes over duty as Adjutant. 2 o.r. demobilised	...

Army Form C. 2118.

WAR DIARY
or
INTELLIGENCE SUMMARY.
(Erase heading not required.)

Instructions regarding War Diaries and Intelligence Summaries are contained in F. S. Regs., Part II. and the Staff Manual respectively. Title pages will be prepared in manuscript.

Place	Date	Hour	Summary of Events and Information	Remarks and references to Appendices
Douai, B.E.	February 1919 14.			
	15	9.45	Coy's usual work. 2nd Lt. R.R. Horton reported to C.L.C. 5 O.R. demobilised	A/101
	16.		Church Parade. S.O.R. demobilised	A/102
	17.		Coy's usual work.	A/103
	18.		Coy's usual work. Major I.T. Evans D.S.O. M.C. takes over 2/c in Command. Capt. Owen C.L. Cmy. L.O.R. demobilised	A/104
	19.		Coy's usual work. 4 O.R. demobilised	A/105
	20.		Lt. Bing and 40 O.R. 'A' Coy. loaded. Lt. Col. W.L. Crawford-James Commdg. Major Ellis 2/c in Command	A/106
			5. O.R. demobilised	A/107
	21.		Coy's usual work. 5 O.R. demobilised	A/108
	22.		Coy's usual work. 4 O.R. demobilised	A/109
	23.	9.45	Church Parade. 2 Lt. A.R. Hickey. - 4 O.R. demobilised	A/110
	24.		Coy's usual work. Following officers: Capt. S.H. Davis M.C., Lt. Y.K. Johns, 2/Lt. A.R. Evans M.C., 2/Lt. V.C. Taylor M.C.	A/111
			2/Lt. W.H. Griffiths and 100 O.R. from 9th Welsh Regt. reported - taken on strength	
	25.		Coy's usual work. 4 O.R. demobilised	A/112
	26.		Coy's usual work. 3 O.R. demobilised	A/113
	27.		Coy's usual work. 1 W.O. and 1 O.R. demobilised	A/114
	28.		Coy's usual work.	A/115
			Coy's usual work. Major A.J. Ellis assumes Command of the Battalion. Capt. Fitzpatrick 2nd in Command. Lt. Col. W.L. Crawford D.S.O. 3 O.R. demobilised	A/116

War Diary
of
6th Bn South Wales Bdrs
for
February 1919

To:- HEADQUARTERS "A"

30th (BRITISH) DIVISION.

Herewith War Diary duly completed for the Month of March, please.

2.4.19.

Major.
Commanding 6th Battalion South Wales Borderers (Pioneers).

Army Form C. 2118.

WAR DIARY
or
INTELLIGENCE SUMMARY.
(Erase heading not required.)

Instructions regarding War Diaries and Intelligence Summaries are contained in F. S. Regs., Part II. and the Staff Manual respectively. Title pages will be prepared in manuscript.

Place	Date	Hour	Summary of Events and Information	Remarks and references to Appendices
Dunkirk	March 1	9.45	Church Parade. Café. 2 o.r. Demobilised.	ind
	2.		A & B Coys manual work at Stosperi & Mardyck Camps. E. Coy bathed	initial
	3.		A & C Coys manual work. D Coy baths. 2 o.r. Demobilised.	initial
	4.		A. C. & D. Coys. usual work. 2 Military medals awarded.	initial
	5.		A C & D Coys usual work. Draft 20 o.r. from 74th Division arrived. 2/Lt W.F. Davis & Lt Roseuyler	initial
			2nd Lt. Harris. G.W. Wybourne. H.C. Price M.C. J. Colfair. M. Hammett. S.C. Hammou Lt S.Tasman	
			from 5th Gurks. Lt F.O. Rogers. 2/Lt H. Barnes.	initial
	6.		A C & D Coys manual work.	initial
	7.		A C & D & Coys Manual work. 2 officers + 100 o.r. proceed to Bergues to work under	initial
	8.	9.45	138th Army Troop Coy. C of E Church Parade.	initial
	9.	R	A C & D. Coys manual work.	initial
	10.		A C & D Coys usual work Transport - L Coy Syncelles Battn.	initial
	11		A C & D Coys usual work.	initial
	12		A & B Coys usual work.	initial
	13		A C & D Coys usual work.	initial
	14		A C & D Coys usual work. 1. o.r. Demobilised	
	15	9.45	C of E Church Service.	

Army Form C. 2118.

WAR DIARY
or
INTELLIGENCE SUMMARY.
(Erase heading not required.)

Place	Date	Hour	Summary of Events and Information	Remarks and references to Appendices
Tunmies	March 16.		E.F. Coys usual work. 'B' Coy baths. D/offr. Lt. W.B. Hough 2/Lt. J.R. Cour 104 O.R. arrived from 24 R.W.F.	JMB
	17		A.F. Coys usual work. 'C' Coy baths.	JMB
	18		A.C. Coys usual work. 'B' Coy baths.	JMB
	19		A.C.F. Coys usual work.	JMB
	20		A.C.F. Coys usual work. D/offr. 26. O.R. arrived from Wendrighe Remounts.	JMB
	21	11:00 hr	C.O.'s Parade.	JMB
	22	9:45	C of E. Parade.	JMB
	23		Coy Parades.	JMB
	24-25		Battalion (less two platoons at Bergues) moved to No 10 Con. Camp EC.AULT.	JMB
Ecault	26		Company Parades.	JMB
	27		Training Parades. A Coy Coys bath.	JMB
	28		Games Parades. Demobilised Capt. Cox. 1 C. 2/Lt. Roy D.	JMB
	29		Games Parades. Award of Decoration Militaire 2nd Class - Croix de Guerre.	JMB
	30	10:00	Church Parade.	JMB
	31		Training Parades.	JMB

Headquarters "A"
30th Division.

6th (3) BATTALION,
SOUTH WALES
BORDERERS (PIONEERS)

No. 310

Herewith War Diary for the month of April 1919.

3.5.1919.
H.W. Dakeyn   Lieut. Colonel.
Commanding 6th Battalion South Wales Borderers (Pioneers).

Army Form C. 2118.

WAR DIARY
INTELLIGENCE SUMMARY.
(Erase heading not required.)

Instructions regarding War Diaries and Intelligence Summaries are contained in F. S. Regs., Part II. and the Staff Manual respectively. Title pages will be prepared in manuscript.

Place	Date	Hour	Summary of Events and Information	Remarks and references to Appendices
ECAULT	APRIL 1		Work as per programme. Inclusion by Colonel Lyon on the ADVANTAGES OF THE POST BELLUM ARMY.	
"	2		Work as per programme.	
"	3		Work as per programme.	
"	4		Work as per programme. Captain (Temp. Lieut. Colonel H.W. DAREWE D.S.O. assumed command of the Bn. vice MAJOR A.J. ELLIS. 2nd Lieut. J.W. NEVILLE took over duties of Messing Officer. 2nd Lieut. H. BARNES, M.M., and 2nd Lieut. P.C. HOLT were posted to 53rd Bn. South Wales Borderers	
"	5		Work as per programme.	
"	6		Captain J.L.C. JONES M.C. assumed command of "A" Coy.. 2/Lt. F. CHAPPELL assumed command of "D" Coy. vice Lieut. R.S. GRIFFITHS demobilized. Church Parade and C.O's inspection of Barracks. 2/Lt. A. ROBERTS demobilized.	
"	7		Work as per programme. 2/Lt. H.L. PRICE assumed duties of M.O. vice Lieut. Offner 2/Lt. O. HART M.C. demobilized.	
"	8		Work as per programme.	
"	9		Work as per programme. Reinforcements - No. 34 5057 R.A.M.S. WHYBROW, and 5 O/R. 4 O/R. demobilized.	
"	10		MAJOR I.T. EVANS D.S.O. M.C. assumed duties of 2nd in command. Work as per programme. 1 O/R demobilized. 2/Lt. R. GREGORY to act as Captain with pay & allowances as Lieut while employed as Adjt. from 3.3.19. Lieut. C.V. CARPENTER rejoined.	
"	11		Work as per programme. 4 O/R demobilized.	
"	12		Work as per programme. Lieut. L.M. DAVIES proceeded to BERGUES to take over command of detachment there.	
"	13		Work as per programme.	
"	14	09.45	Divine service.	
"	15		Work as per programme. 2/Lt. R. HAMMETT assumed duties of A/Adjt during absence of Lieut. GREGORY on leave. 2/Lt. H. PRICE. M.C. assumed command of H.Q. vice 2/Lt. J.S.W. NEVILLE demobilized. Lieut. F.O. ROGERS posted to 53rd Bn. S.W. Borderers. Reinforcements 3 O/R. 2 O/R demobilized.	

Army Form C. 2118.

WAR DIARY 6/S.W.B.
or
INTELLIGENCE SUMMARY. 2/2
(Erase heading not required.)

Instructions regarding War Diaries and Intelligence Summaries are contained in F. S. Regs., Part II. and the Staff Manual respectively. Title pages will be prepared in manuscript.

Place	Date	Hour	Summary of Events and Information	Remarks and references to Appendices
ECAULT.	APRIL 16		Work as per programme. 1°/R. demobilized.	aq.2
"	17		Work as per programme.	aq.1
"	18	10.30	Divine Service. Reinforcements. 1 h. O/R. 2/Lt W.S. SMYTH posted to 5/32 Bn. S.W.B. 6 O/R. emlisted to D.R.	aq.2
"	19		Work as per programme. Reinforcements 20 O/R. 2/Lt R.W.F. 9 O/R. 25 th R.W.F.	aq.2
"	20	10.30	Divine Service.	aq.2
"	21		Holiday.	aq.1
"	22		Rest work. Reinforcements 3 O/R. 1 O/R demobilized.	aq.5
"	23	08.00	Work as per programme. Reinforcements. 2/Lt W.C. FLEMING, Cheshire Regt. 2/Lt R.W. LEVICK. S.W.B. 2/Lt L.I. SHEPHEARD. Cheshire Regt. 1 O/R demobilized.	aq.2
"	24		Work as per programme. 1°/R. demobilized.	aq.2
"	25		Work as per programme.	aq.2
"	26		Work as per programme. Reinforcements 4 O/R. 3 Officers & 6 O/R. rejoined from BERGUES.	aq.2
"	27	09.30	Divine Service.	aq.1
"	28		Work as per programme.	aq.1
"	29		Work as per programme.	aq.2
"	30		Work as per programme. 2/Lt. S.J. SHEPHEARD appointed Bn. L.G. Officer. Reinforcements 24 O/R. 2 O/R. 3rd Bn.	aq.2
			Captain H. STONEMAN. M.C. assumes command 7 D 65.	aq.1

A.W. Bakewell
Lt. Colonel
COMMANDING 6th (SERV) Bn. S.W. BORDERERS.

WAR DIARY
or
INTELLIGENCE SUMMARY.

Army Form C. 2118.

6/S.W. Borderers 2/3

A.100.
Date 5/6/19

Place	Date	Hour	Summary of Events and Information	Remarks and references to Appendices
ECAULT	May 1		Usual Parade.	O.C.
"	2		Route march.	O.C.
"	3		Usual Parade.	O.C.
"	4	10.00	Divine Service.	O.C.
"	5		Usual Parade.	O.C.
"	6		Usual Parade.	O.C.
"	7		Usual Parade.	O.C.
"	8		Usual Parade.	O.C.
"	9		Usual Parade.	O.C.
"	10		Usual Parade.	O.C.
"	11	11.30	Divine Service.	O.C.
"	12		Usual Parade. Lieut. T. N. Johns Lieut. J. C. L. VAUGHAN, M.C. joined the Battn.	O.C.
"	13		Usual Parade.	O.C.
"	14		Route March. 4 O/R demobilized.	O.C.
"	15		Usual Parade. 10/R reinforcement.	O.C.
"	16		Usual Parade. Lieut. E.A.C. Jones rejoined.	O.C.
"	17		Usual Parade.	O.C.
"	18	10.30	Divine Service. 2 O/R reinforcement.	O.C.
"	19		Usual Parade.	O.C.
"	20		Usual Parade. Withdrawn by G.O.C. 2 Lieut. F.J. SHEPHEARD demobilized.	O.C.

WAR DIARY 6/S.W.Borderers
or
INTELLIGENCE SUMMARY

Army Form C. 2118.

Place	Date	Hour	Summary of Events and Information	Remarks and references to Appendices
ECAULT	MAY. 21		Usual Parades. 4 O/Rs demobilized.	a/s.
"	22		Route march.	a/s.
"	23		Usual Parades. No. 46959 C&MS JAMES D.A. and 1 O/R demobilized.	a/s.
"	24		Usual Parades. Divisional Sports in afternoon. 3 O/Rs reinforcements.	a/s.
"	25	9.30	Parade in full marching order.	a/s.
		10.30	Divine Service. 1 O/R demobilized. 2nd Lieut. H.L. PRICE. M.C. rejoined.	a/s.
"	26		Usual Parades. 1 O/R reinforcement.	a/s.
"	27		Usual Parades.	a/s.
"	28		Usual Parades. 4 O/Rs demobilized.	a/s.
"	29		Usual Parades.	a/s.
"	30	8.30	Route march.	a/s.
"	31		Usual Parade. 1 O/R reinforcement.	a/s.

A.L. Sahyn
LT. COLONEL
COMMANDING 6th (SER.) Bn. S.W. BORDERERS

War Diary
of
6th S W B
for
May 1919

WAR DIARY

6th South Wales Borderers

Army Form C. 2118.

Instructions regarding War Diaries and Intelligence Summaries are contained in F.S. Regs., Part II. and the Staff Manual respectively. Title pages will be prepared in manuscript.

INTELLIGENCE SUMMARY
(Erase heading not required.)

Place	Date	Hour	Summary of Events and Information	Remarks and references to Appendices
ECAULT	JUNE 1st	9 am	Commanding Officers Parade.	
"	2	15.30	Consecration Presentation of the "King's Colours". Presentation by Maj. Gen. T.D. Jeffreys C.B. C.M.G.	
"	3		Manual Parades. The following were awarded the M.S.M. 1/15392 R.S.M. Penven G. (W.O.II) 6/9647 C.S.M. Rosevear S. (W.O.II)	
			263156 R.Q.M.S. Hybart A. 2 Lt. (Sr. Sgt) R.W.T. 2nd Lt Ball joined Battn. from 8th South Staff Reg	
			The following officers were demobilised 2nd Lt. G.V. Carpenter, 2nd Lt. R.W. Levick, 2nd Lt.S.B. Emmott 2nd Lt Aet. Smyth M.M.	
"	4th		Detachment from the Battn. relieved detachments of the 30th Battn. M.G.C. at the following places.	
			"A" Coy. No 3 Rest Camp. Daily duties. Field Punishment Bonfire.	
			" — " — " Police Detention	
			"B" Coy. Bassin Loubet.	
			"D" Coy. Colour Camp. A.S.C. School of Cookery. OUTREAU & PONT DE BRIQUES	
		5th	2nd Lt Chappell & 2nd Lt Mount relieved officers of the 30th Battn. M.G.C. at AIRE & FAUQUEMBERGUES	
			Officers Instructional classes. Lectures by Commanding Officer. Remainder of Oths on Fatigues.	
		6th	2nd Lt. Ravenscroft assumes duties of Transport Officer. 7 OR's Reinforcements	
			The Battn. relieved the 30th Battn. M.G.C. at HENRIVILLE CAMP. The 30th M.G.C. army of the 6 ECAULT	
			2nd Lt. R. Griffiths carried the colours	
HENRIVILLE CAMP.	7th		All Drafts & Daily duties for BOULOGNE Base moved at 18.30 hours daily.	

47.S.
H.M.

WAR DIARY or INTELLIGENCE SUMMARY

Army Form C. 2118.

6th South Wales Borderers

(Erase heading not required.)

Place	Date	Hour	Summary of Events and Information	Remarks and references to Appendices
HENRIVILLE CAMP	5th		Two R.O.R. proceeded for duty to the Chinese Depot NOYELLES. Major A.J. Elliot proceeded to England.	
"	6th		Voluntary services were held for the C. of E. Roman Catholic & others in service.	
"	7th		Whit Monday. The day was observed as a holiday.	
"	8th		2nd Lt. Hammett proceeded to ROUEN Ordnance Depot. 2 O.R.s rejoined the battn from Hospital.	
"	9th		Officers Instructional classes. Lecture by Capt. R.L. Jones M.C. All O.R.s parade for fatigues. Lewis Gun classes parade under 2nd Lt. Inf. Smith.	
"	10th		Parades as above. Lecture by the Commanding Officer.	
"	11th		Parades as above. 5 O.R.s rejoined the battn from 69th Inf. Bde. H.Q.	
"	12th		Parades as above. Lecture by Lt. T.H. Johns.	
"	13th		Parades as above. Lecture by Capt. H. Chapman M.C.	
"	14th		Voluntary divine services held at Prince's BEATRICE HUT. also service for R.C. 2 O.R.s proceeded to UK for demobilisation. 4 O.R.s struck off strength, transferred to 229 Emp. Coy.	
"	15th		Officers Instructional classes. Lecture by Lieut G.J.L. Huggan M.C. All O.R.s parade for fatigues.	
"	16th		Parades as above. Lecture by 2nd Lt. R. Griffith. 16 O.R.s proceeded to Hire on detachment. Extract from London Gazette. "Order of the British Empire" bestowed upon T/Lt. Col. J. Capt. R. Lees 6th S.W.B. in recognition of valuable services rendered in France & Flanders. 2 O.R.s reinforcements.	

WAR DIARY 6th Batt K.O.S. Borderers. Army Form C. 2118.
or
INTELLIGENCE SUMMARY.
(Erase heading not required.)

Place	Date	Hour	Summary of Events and Information	Remarks and references to Appendices
HENRIVILLE CAMP	17th		Officers Instructional classes. Lecture by 2nd Lt. G. Wybourn. All Others handed to fatigues.	
"			2 Others Reinforcements. 2 Others struck off strength.	
"			2nd Lt. B. Williamson (6th Batt) appointed bomb Instructor officer DUNKERQUE BASE. Lt-Col H.Y. Smyth appointed	
"	18th		Parade as above	
"	19th		Parade as above. Lecture by 2nd Lt. A.S. Greene	
"	20		Parade as above " Lt. E.R.C. Frackham. 5 Others reinforcements	
"	21st		4 Others struck off strength of Batt. 2 Others Reinforcements. 1 Other reinforcement	
"			Following Officers left with the Princess Beatrice Batt:-	
"			Lt. Col. Davies evacuated to U.K. 3 Others struck off strength	
"			Capt. 2nd Lieuts to be 1/Lieuts Lt. R.C. Greer (July 19.17) & Ravenscroft (May 28th).	
"	22nd		Officers Instructional classes. Lecture by Lieut. M.R. Evans M.C. All Others handed to fatigues	
"	23rd		Parade as above. Lecture by Lieut. E.B.T. Loring Thomas	
"	24th		Parade as above. 1 Other Reinforcement.	
"	25th		Parade as above. Lecture by 2nd Lt. C. Stoppes.	
"	26th		Parade as above. 2nd Lt. M.B. Griffiths proceeds 4 hours to the presbytère at Wimeneux Officer	
"			The Battn supplied 112 men for an Inter Allies Torchlight procession to Boulogne	

WAR DIARY
or
INTELLIGENCE SUMMARY

1st South Wales Borderers Army Form C. 2118.

(Erase heading not required.)

Place	Date	Hour	Summary of Events and Information	Remarks and references to Appendices
HENRIVILLE CAMP	27th		Church as above. Lecture by Rev. E. E. Davies. "On Worship"	
"	28th		Holiday	
"	29th		Voluntary Services. The 30th Divisional Mounted Sports took place	
"	30th		Officers Instructional classes. Lecture by Capt. Rd. Griffiths M.C. 2nd R.W.Fusiliers	

A. W. Bateson
LT. COLONEL
COMMANDING 6TH (SER.) Bn. S.W. BORDERERS

War Diary

of

6th Bn South Wales
Borderers

for

June 1919.

www.ingramcontent.com/pod-product-compliance
Lightning Source LLC
Chambersburg PA
CBHW081445160426
43193CB00013B/2385